I0422984

HOLIDAY SURVIVAL GUIDE

Jingle Bright, Spend Light, Sleigh Bells Over Inflation's Height

"Amid the winter's snow and lights, the holidays remind us that warmth is not found in things, but in the hearts of those we hold close."

Dobbs Media

Jingle Bright, Spend Light, Sleigh Bells Over Inflation's Height

The holidays can be stressful even under the best of circumstances, but with rising inflation and financial constraints, they can feel downright daunting. However, with a bit of planning, creativity, and resilience, you can enjoy the holiday spirit without breaking the bank.

Table of Contents

Plan Ahead

The value of planning ahead, especially when navigating the holiday season on a tight budget, cannot be overemphasized. Here's a detailed breakdown of why this is crucial and how you can effectively do it:

Why Plan Ahead?

1. **Financial Predictability**: Knowing how much you intend to spend in total and per item or activity allows you to avoid unexpected financial surprises.

2. **Reduced Stress**: Last-minute shopping or arrangements can be hectic and stressful. Planning ahead allows for a more relaxed holiday experience.

3. **Better Choices**: Giving yourself more time to make decisions can result in better, more thoughtful purchases or plans.

4. **Avoiding the Last-Minute Premium**: Retailers are aware that last-minute shoppers can be

desperate. As a result, many discounts are available earlier in the season.

Steps to Effective Planning:

1. **Start Early**: Ideally, begin your holiday planning a few months in advance. This doesn't necessarily mean buying gifts in July, but it does mean setting a clear timeline and sticking to it.

2. **List Everything Out**: Break down your holiday needs:

   - **Gifts**: Who are you buying for? What's your budget for each person?

   - **Food**: Are you hosting any meals or parties? What will you need to buy?

   - **Travel**: If you're traveling, factor in costs such as gas, tickets, accommodation, and so on.

   - **Decorations**: Do you need to buy any new decorations or can you reuse last year's?

   - **Miscellaneous**: Always have a small budget for unexpected costs.

3. **Research**: Once you have your lists:

   - Look up potential gifts online to get an idea of costs.

   - Explore bulk deals for food or decorations.

   - Check for early-bird deals on travel tickets or accommodations.

4. **Set Up Alerts**: Many online platforms offer price drop notifications. If you've eyed a particular product, set up an alert so you get notified when it's on sale.

5. **Spread Out Purchases**: You don't need to buy everything at once. In fact, spreading out your purchases can help you manage your cash flow better. Buy a few items every week or every paycheck.

6. **Track Expenditures**: Keep a record of every holiday-related expense. This not only ensures you stay within budget but also helps in planning for the next year.

7. **Consider Layaway**: Some stores offer layaway plans which allow you to select items and pay

for them over time. This can be a useful way to secure a popular item and pay for it in increments.

8. **DIY & Handmade**: Planning ahead gives you the time to craft DIY gifts or decorations. Often, these can be more meaningful and cost-effective than store-bought alternatives.

9. **Plan for Next Year**: It might sound over-the-top, but once this holiday season is over, start thinking about the next one. Some post-holiday sales offer deep discounts, making it a good time to snag deals for the following year.

In essence, planning ahead for the holiday season is all about preparation, research, and thoughtful decision-making. By taking the time to plan out each aspect of your holiday spending, you can enjoy the festive season without the financial strain.

Set a Budget

Setting a budget is fundamental in ensuring that the festive season doesn't lead you into financial turmoil. Let's delve deeper into the process of creating and sticking to a holiday budget:

Why Set a Budget?

1. **Financial Control**: A budget is your roadmap. It ensures you don't overspend, accumulate debt, or tap into funds reserved for other essentials like bills or rent.

2. **Mental Peace**: Knowing that you're operating within a set financial boundary can alleviate the anxiety associated with unplanned expenditures.

3. **Prioritization**: A budget helps you allocate funds to what matters most, ensuring that the most important aspects of your holiday get the attention (and funds) they deserve.

Steps to Setting a Robust Budget:

1. **Determine Overall Spending Limit**:

   - Analyze your financial situation: Review your savings, income, and expected expenses.

   - Decide on a total amount you're comfortable spending without impacting your financial stability.

2. **Itemize and Categorize**:

   - **Gifts**: List out everyone you intend to buy for, and allocate a specific amount for each.

   - **Food**: Estimate the cost of holiday meals, parties, and any additional festive treats.

   - **Decorations**: Do an inventory of what you already have and decide if new purchases are necessary.

   - **Travel**: Factor in fuel, accommodation, meals, and any other related expenses.

- **Miscellaneous**: Set aside a portion for unforeseen expenses. This could be for last-minute gifts, higher-than-expected shipping fees, or other surprise costs.

3. **Be Realistic**: Ensure the amounts allocated are reasonable. It's better to overestimate slightly and have a surplus than to underestimate and end up overspending.

4. **Adjust and Balance**: If your estimated costs exceed your overall spending limit, make adjustments. This might mean cutting back on certain categories or re-evaluating your priorities.

5. **Track as You Spend**: Each time you make a holiday-related purchase, subtract it from the relevant category in your budget. There are many budgeting apps available that can assist with this, or you can use a simple spreadsheet or even pen and paper.

6. **Avoid Impulse Purchases**: Only buy what you've budgeted for. If you come across an unplanned

purchase, see if you can adjust other parts of your budget to accommodate it.

7. **Review and Adjust**: Midway through the season, review your budget. If you've spent more in one category, see if you can balance it out by cutting back in another.

8. **Consider Alternative Payment Methods**: If you're worried about overspending, consider using cash or prepaid cards for holiday purchases. It's harder to go over budget when the money is physically leaving your wallet, or when you have a set amount on a card.

9. **Post-Holiday Reflection**: Once the season is over, review your budget. Analyze where you overspent, what you saved on, and use this as a learning experience for the next holiday season.

Remember, the essence of setting a budget is not about restriction but about making informed choices. When done correctly, it empowers you to celebrate the holidays in a way that is both enjoyable and financially sound.

Prioritize Experiences Over Things: The Value of Creating Memories

In an era of consumerism, where the emphasis often lies on the material, pivoting towards experiences can be both refreshing and fulfilling. Let's explore why prioritizing experiences over tangible items can be more meaningful and how you can integrate this approach into your holidays.

Why Choose Experiences Over Things?

1. **Lasting Memories**: Physical gifts can wear out, get lost, or become outdated. In contrast, memories from experiences last a lifetime and often grow fonder with time.

2. **Deepen Relationships**: Shared experiences can strengthen bonds, allowing you to connect on a deeper level with loved ones.

3. **Personal Growth**: Experiences often lead to learning and personal development. They can

provide new perspectives, skills, or insights about oneself and others.

4. **Avoid Clutter**: Shifting from physical gifts can also be a step towards minimalism, reducing the clutter in one's living space.

5. **Value Over Price**: Often, the cost of an experience doesn't directly correlate with its value. Simple, low-cost experiences can be as, if not more, fulfilling than extravagant ones.

Ideas for Experience-Based Gifts and Traditions:

1. **Homemade Coupons**: Create personalized coupons for loved ones. These can include:

   - A picnic day at the park.

   - An evening of board games and snacks.

   - A day where they choose all activities.

   - A homemade dinner of their choice.

2. **Promise of Quality Time**: In today's busy world, simply giving someone your undivided attention can be a priceless gift. Plan a day where you spend time together without distractions—no

phones, no TV, just quality conversation and bonding.

3. **DIY Projects**: Choose a project that you can work on together. This can be:

   - Crafting a scrapbook of your shared memories.

   - Building something functional for the home.

   - Gardening or creating a small home vegetable patch.

   - Learning and practicing a new hobby together, like pottery or painting.

4. **Gift Classes or Workshops**: Enroll in a class based on the recipient's interest. This can be dance classes, pottery workshops, cooking classes, or any other skill they've shown interest in.

5. **Plan a Staycation**: Explore your city or town as a tourist. Visit local attractions, museums, or parks. Sometimes, amazing experiences await right on our doorsteps.

6. **Start a Book Club**: For the literature lover, start a family or friend book club where you read and discuss a new book every month.

7. **Camping Night**: If you have a backyard, set up a tent and have a camping night complete with a bonfire, marshmallow roasting, and stargazing.

8. **Customized Experiences**: Tailor experiences based on the individual. For a music lover, perhaps plan a day to explore new music genres together. For someone who loves cooking, try cooking a new cuisine together.

9. **Memory Jar**: Start a new tradition where you write down good things that happen throughout the year and store them in a jar. During the holiday season, sit together and read them aloud.

10.   **Recurring Experiences**: Create traditions that occur annually. This gives everyone something to look forward to and can form the backbone of cherished memories over the years.

When you prioritize experiences over things, you're choosing depth, connection, and lasting memories over temporary satisfaction. Especially in times of financial strain, focusing on experiences can be a fulfilling way to celebrate the holiday spirit without the emphasis on materialism.

DIY Gifts: Crafting Meaningful Moments with Handmade Treasures

In a world often dominated by store-bought presents, DIY gifts emerge as sincere, heartfelt tokens of love. They not only allow for personal touches but can also be a more economical way to convey appreciation. Let's delve into the world of DIY gifts, their significance, and ideas to inspire your creativity.

Why Choose DIY Gifts?

1. **Personal Touch**: Handmade gifts carry a part of the giver with them. They represent time, effort, and thought, making them exceptionally special.

2. **Cost-Effective**: While some DIY projects can be intricate, many are economical, utilizing materials you might already have or ones that are relatively cheap to procure.

3. **Unique and One-of-a-Kind**: Unlike mass-produced items, your DIY gift is unique. There won't be another one quite like it anywhere.

4. **Flexibility**: You can tailor your gift to the recipient's tastes and preferences, ensuring they receive something they'll truly love.

5. **Eco-Friendly**: Many DIY gifts can be made from recycled or sustainable materials, reducing the environmental footprint of your gift.

Inspiring Ideas for DIY Gifts:

1. **Crafts**:

- **Personalized Mugs**: With porcelain markers or paints, you can create custom designs on plain ceramic mugs.
- **Beaded Jewelry**: Make personalized necklaces, bracelets, or earrings.
- **Photo Coasters**: Using tiles, photos, and some resin or mod podge, craft coasters that feature cherished memories.

2. **Baked Goods**:

- **Cookies or Brownies**: Present them in a decorative tin or box for added flair.
- **Homemade Jams and Preserves**: Package in a glass jar with a ribbon and label.
- **DIY Recipe Kit**: Include all the dry ingredients for a special cookie or cake recipe in a jar, with instructions attached.

3. **Handwritten Gifts**:

- **Letters**: Pour your heart out and recount shared memories, express gratitude, or envision a shared future.
- **Poetry or Short Stories**: Write a personal poem or a story featuring the recipient.
- **Recipe Book**: Compile family recipes or ones you've created together, and craft a homemade recipe book.

4. **Home & Garden**:

- **Hand-painted Plant Pots**: Add a plant for an extra touch.
- **Scented Candles**: Customize with their favorite scents.

- **Homemade Soap or Bath Bombs**: Personalize with scents, colors, and shapes they'd adore.

5. **Personal Care**:

- **DIY Scrubs**: Combine sugar or salt with oils and essential oils for a simple yet luxurious scrub.
- **Lip Balms**: Using beeswax, oils, and maybe a hint of tint or flavor.
- **Handmade Lotion Bars**: Crafted with shea butter, coconut oil, and beeswax, these are great for dry winter skin.

6. **Memory Collections**:

- **Scrapbooks**: Chronicle your shared moments, complete with pictures, tickets, and other memorabilia.
- **Playlists**: Compile a list of songs that remind you of them or your shared moments.
- **Video Messages**: Collect video messages from friends and family to surprise the recipient.

7. **Learning Kits**:

- **DIY Craft Kits**: Assemble all the essentials for a specific craft or art project, complete with instructions.
- **Grow Kits**: Include seeds, a small pot, and instructions for them to grow their plant.

8. **For the Book Lover**:

- **Personalized Bookmarks**: Crafted from paper, leather, or even metal.
- **Hand-bound Journals**: For them to pen down their thoughts.

Remember, the beauty of DIY gifts lies in the process as much as the result. Each step of creation embeds your love, care, and attention into the gift. So even if you're not a master craftsman or a baking genius, the sincerity behind a handmade gift often shines brighter than any price tag.

Re-Gift Thoughtfully

Re-gifting, the practice of passing on an unused or unwanted gift to someone else, is becoming an increasingly accepted custom. When done with discretion and thoughtfulness, it can be a savvy way to ensure that items don't go to waste. Let's dive into how to navigate the waters of re-gifting without stepping on any toes.

Why Re-Gift?

1. **Eco-Friendly**: Instead of discarding unwanted items, you give them a new life and reduce waste.

2. **Budget-Friendly**: In tight financial situations, re-gifting can be a practical solution.

3. **Decluttering**: Instead of letting unused items take up space, you can pass them on to someone who might cherish them.

4. **Gift Suitability**: Sometimes, a gift that doesn't resonate with you might be the perfect fit for someone else.

Rules and Tips for Thoughtful Re-Gifting:

1. **Ensure the Item is New and Unused**: Only re-gift items that are in pristine condition. The item should ideally still be in its original packaging.

2. **Remember the Original Giver**: As the old adage goes, "It's the thought that counts." Recognize the intent of the original giver and ensure they won't be in a situation where they realize you've re-gifted their present. Make a note to remember who gifted you the item to avoid potential awkward situations.

3. **Consider the Recipient**: Re-gifting shouldn't be about simply passing on unwanted items. Think about whether the gift genuinely aligns with the recipient's tastes or needs.

4. **Repackage If Necessary**: Fresh wrapping paper and a new card can breathe new life into a gift. Ensure that there are no old notes, cards, or any other personalized tags from the original gifting.

5. **Avoid Re-Gifting within the Same Circle**: It's risky to re-gift within the same social or family

circle. There's always the chance the original giver could find out, leading to potential discomfort or hurt feelings.

6. **Stay Away from Personalized or Handmade Items**: Anything that was personalized or crafted specifically for you shouldn't be re-gifted. It would be quite evident, and it can come across as highly inconsiderate.

7. **Be Honest If Caught**: On the off chance that someone does find out about the re-gift, it's essential to be honest. Acknowledge it gracefully, emphasizing your desire for the item to be genuinely appreciated and loved.

8. **Evaluate Frequency**: If you find yourself consistently considering re-gifting items from a particular person, it might be worth having an open conversation with them about gift preferences or even suggesting non-material ways of showing appreciation.

9. **Don't Re-Gift Just to Do It**: The goal should always be thoughtfulness. If you're re-gifting

solely to fulfill a gift-giving obligation without considering the recipient, it's better to refrain.

10.   **Keep Feelings in Mind**: Always be sensitive to feelings—both of the person who originally gave you the gift and the person you're giving it to. It's essential to navigate re-gifting with empathy.

In conclusion, while re-gifting can be a practical and eco-friendly solution, it requires careful consideration. When done right, it ensures that items are loved and appreciated rather than gathering dust. However, it's essential to approach the practice with a genuine spirit of giving, ensuring the choice benefits the recipient and maintains the integrity of gift-giving traditions.

Take Advantage of Sales and Discounts

Sales events, from Black Friday to end-of-season clearances, can be a shopper's dream. They offer the allure of quality products at a fraction of the regular price. However, amidst the buzz and excitement, it's essential to differentiate between genuine bargains and mere marketing gimmicks.

Why Shop During Sales?

1. **Significant Savings**: Major sales events can offer considerable discounts, allowing you to buy quality products at a much-reduced price.

2. **Budget-Friendly**: For those living paycheck to paycheck, waiting for these sales can be a strategic way to maximize a tight budget, especially during the holiday season.

3. **Bulk Purchases**: Sales are often a good time to buy in bulk, especially for non-perishable items or gifts you can give throughout the year.

Strategies to Shop Smart During Sales:

1. **Research in Advance**: Before the sale begins, identify what you need. Create a wish list and stick to it to avoid impulse purchases.

2. **Set a Budget**: Just because items are discounted doesn't mean you should buy indiscriminately. Determine a budget for your shopping spree and stick to it.

3. **Compare Prices**: Check the regular prices of items beforehand to ensure the discount is genuine. Use price comparison tools or apps to see if the "sale" price is truly a bargain.

4. **Check Return Policies**: Some discounted items may have a "no return" or "final sale" policy. Make sure you're comfortable with the return conditions before purchasing.

5. **Prioritize Quality Over Quantity**: A low price doesn't always equate to a good deal. Ensure that the products you're buying are of good quality and have good reviews.

6. **Beware of Doorbusters**: These are deeply discounted items meant to draw shoppers into the store. They're often limited in quantity and can be of lesser quality. Determine if it's truly a bargain or just a tactic to lure you in.

7. **Shop Online**: Many deals are available online, saving you the hassle of fighting through crowds. Plus, it's easier to compare prices and read reviews.

8. **Utilize Price Drop Refunds**: Some credit cards or stores offer a price drop refund if an item you purchased drops in price within a certain timeframe. Check if this applies to your purchases.

9. **Limit "Buy More, Save More" Deals**: While offers like "buy one get one free" or "spend $100 and get $20 off" sound appealing, ensure you're not buying more than you need just to get a deal.

10. **Avoid Opening Store Credit Cards for Discounts**: Many stores offer an additional discount if you open a credit card with them.

While tempting, these cards often come with high interest rates that can cost you more in the long run if you don't pay the balance in full.

11.   **Read Reviews**: Before buying, especially electronics or appliances, read reviews to ensure you're getting a quality product. Just because it's on sale doesn't mean it's worth buying.

12.   **Check for Coupons**: Even during a sale, there might be additional coupons or promotional codes available online. Before checking out, do a quick search.

13.   **Stay Updated**: Sign up for newsletters or follow your favorite stores on social media. This way, you'll be alerted to flash sales or additional discounts.

14.   **Avoid Extended Warranties**: Salespeople often push extended warranties during sales, but these are rarely worth the cost. Most products come with a manufacturer's warranty that's sufficient.

In conclusion, while sales and discounts can provide excellent opportunities to save, it's crucial to shop with discernment. By being well-informed, setting a budget, and avoiding marketing traps, you can ensure that you're truly getting the most value for your money.

Opt for Potluck Gatherings: Celebrating Togetherness and Affordability

In the midst of rising costs and tight budgets, potluck gatherings stand out as a symbol of community and shared responsibility. They remind us that the essence of celebrations lies in togetherness, and not just in extravagant displays. Here's a detailed look into why and how potluck gatherings can be both meaningful and economical.

Why Choose Potluck Gatherings?

1. **Shared Financial Burden**: Instead of one person or family bearing the entire expense, everyone contributes, making it lighter on individual pockets.

2. **Variety of Dishes**: A potluck naturally brings a diverse range of dishes to the table, ensuring there's something for everyone's palate.

3. **Showcasing Talent**: Everyone gets a chance to showcase their culinary skills or share a special family recipe.

4. **Building Community**: Contributing to a meal fosters a sense of community, belonging, and shared celebration.

5. **Less Stress for the Host**: The host doesn't need to cater to everyone's dietary preferences and restrictions, as guests typically bring what they'd prefer to eat.

Tips for Organizing a Successful Potluck Gathering:

1. **Coordinate in Advance**: Use group chats, emails, or potluck apps to coordinate who's bringing what. This ensures a balanced meal with a mix of appetizers, main courses, sides, and desserts.

2. **Set a Theme**: Give your potluck a theme, be it ethnic cuisines, comfort foods, or even dishes from a particular decade. It adds fun and ensures some cohesiveness in the menu.

3. **Be Inclusive**: Be aware of dietary restrictions, allergies, or preferences like vegetarian, vegan, gluten-free, etc. Encourage guests to label their dishes accordingly.

4. **Consider Logistics**: Ensure there's enough fridge space, oven availability (for reheating), and serving dishes/utensils for everyone's contributions.

5. **Encourage Reusable Containers**: Advocate for sustainability by suggesting guests bring their dishes in reusable containers.

6. **Supply Basics**: As the host, it's a good idea to provide basic items like drinks, ice, plates, utensils, and napkins, unless you've coordinated for others to bring them.

7. **Recipe Exchange**: If a dish becomes a hit, it's always fun to exchange recipes. Consider creating a shared document or group where attendees can upload their recipes after the event.

8. **Acknowledge Efforts**: Take a moment to acknowledge everyone's efforts and express

gratitude. It makes contributors feel valued and appreciated.

9. **Leftovers**: Plan for leftovers. Encourage guests to bring take-away containers or have some available so that everyone can take a portion of the remaining dishes.

10.   **Safety First**: Especially important in warmer seasons or climates, ensure that dishes, especially those with dairy or meat, don't sit out too long. It's always good to have coolers or warming trays handy.

11.   **Activities**: Beyond just food, think of activities or games that guests can partake in. It could be something that complements the theme of your potluck.

12.   **Beverages**: While guests can bring dishes, it might be easier for the host to manage beverages. From soft drinks to adult beverages, consider what would best complement the meal.

Potluck gatherings embody the proverb, "It takes a village." They remind us that celebrations are richer when everyone chips in, not just in terms of food, but in terms of love, effort, and the shared joy of being together. Amidst economic pressures, such gatherings underscore the importance of community and the simple pleasures of shared meals.

Limit Travel: Nurturing Connections in an Inflationary Climate

When financial challenges loom, and the costs of travel soar, it might seem like our connections with distant loved ones are at risk. However, in today's digital age, geography no longer dictates the depth or quality of our relationships. By rethinking our approach to travel and utilizing available resources, we can still foster meaningful connections without breaking the bank.

Why Limit Travel?

1. **Cost Savings**: At a time when every penny counts, avoiding high airline tickets or gas prices can result in significant savings.

2. **Environmental Considerations**: Reducing travel, especially by air or car, lowers our carbon footprint, making our holidays more eco-friendly.

3. **Stress Reduction**: Avoiding the rush and stress of holiday travel, last-minute ticket bookings, and potential delays can make your holiday season more peaceful and restorative.

Alternatives to Traditional Travel:

1. **Virtual Gatherings**: With platforms like Zoom, Skype, FaceTime, and Microsoft Teams, you can have face-to-face interactions with loved ones. Consider setting a date and time for a virtual family gathering where everyone tunes in for a collective chat.

2. **Virtual Tours**: Spend a day exploring a place together virtually. Many museums, historical sites, and even national parks offer virtual tours. This can be a unique way to 'travel' together without leaving your home.

3. **Shared Activities**: Engage in activities simultaneously and then share experiences. This could be as simple as watching the same movie or cooking the same recipe and then discussing it.

4. **Snail Mail**: Rediscover the joy of handwritten letters. There's something deeply personal about receiving a tangible note of love and care.

5. **Plan for Off-Peak Travel**: If you still wish to travel, consider doing so during off-peak times when costs might be lower. This could be after major holidays or during weekdays.

6. **Local Explorations**: Become a tourist in your own city or locality. Explore local parks, museums, or new places you haven't been to. This fulfills the desire for novelty and exploration without the hefty price tag of distant travel.

7. **Staycations**: Rather than venturing out, create a holiday environment at home. This could involve setting up a camping tent in your backyard, having themed dinners, or dedicating a weekend to reading or movie marathons.

8. **Gift Experiences**: Instead of physical gifts, consider gifting experiences. This could be an online course, a subscription to a magazine or

streaming service, or even tickets to a local event.

9. **Recorded Messages**: Send loved ones a video or voice message capturing special moments, insights, or simply a heartfelt message. This can often feel more personal than a standard phone call.

10. **Collaborative Projects**: Engage in collaborative projects like family books, scrapbooks, or online blogs where everyone contributes memories, photos, and stories.

The essence of holidays and connections isn't in the distance traveled but in the depth of connection shared. By embracing the available tools and technologies, and sometimes revisiting older, more traditional forms of communication, we can bridge any geographical divide. It's a gentle reminder that the heart doesn't count miles; it counts moments.

Secret Santa: A Thoughtful and Economical Gift-Giving Tradition

In larger groups, be it family gatherings, workplace parties, or friend circles, gift-giving can be a daunting and expensive task. Everyone wants to express appreciation and love, but buying gifts for everyone might stretch the budget too thin, especially during economically challenging times. Enter the tradition of Secret Santa—a solution that's both festive and financially mindful.

Why Opt for Secret Santa?

1. **Budget-Friendly**: By buying for just one person, you can allocate a reasonable budget and stick to it without feeling the pressure to purchase multiple gifts.

2. **Thoughtful Gifting**: With only one gift to focus on, you can invest time in choosing something meaningful and tailored to that individual's preferences or needs.

3. **Simplified Shopping**: The holiday shopping frenzy can be overwhelming. Secret Santa

narrows down your shopping list, making the experience more enjoyable and less chaotic.

4. **Excitement and Anticipation**: The surprise element—both in terms of who your Secret Santa is and what gift you'll receive—adds a layer of fun and suspense to the holiday celebrations.

Organizing a Successful Secret Santa:

1. **Draw Names Early**: Whether you're using physical names in a hat or one of the many online Secret Santa generators, ensure this is done well in advance to give participants ample time to shop.

2. **Set a Budget**: Decide on a budget that's comfortable for all participants. This ensures everyone's gifts are roughly in the same price range, keeping things fair.

3. **Wish Lists**: Encourage participants to create wish lists or provide some hints. This aids the Secret Santa in choosing a gift that's likely to be appreciated.

4. **Emphasize Thoughtfulness**: Remind participants that it's the thought behind the gift that counts, not the price tag. Handmade or personalized gifts can be especially touching.

5. **Gift Exchange Event**: Plan a specific time for the gift exchange, whether it's at a holiday party or a designated gathering. The reveal of both the gift and the identity of each Secret Santa is a highlight.

6. **Anonymous Notes**: Allow Secret Santas to leave anonymous notes or hints leading up to the gift exchange, adding to the mystery and anticipation.

7. **Online Shopping and Direct Delivery**: For groups that can't meet in person, participants can shop online and have the gift directly delivered to the recipient's address.

8. **Themes**: To add a twist, consider setting a theme for the gifts—like "books," "handmade," "local products," or "gifts under $10."

9. **Homemade Gifts**: Encourage crafting or homemade gifts. These can be more heartfelt and often cost less than store-bought items.

10.   **Charitable Twist**: If everyone in the group agrees, you can have a version where the gifts are donations to each person's favorite charity.

11.   **Reveal Option**: Some groups like to keep the Secret Santa anonymous even after the gift is opened, while others enjoy the big reveal. Decide as a group which option you'll follow.

12.   **Regifting**: If it's agreeable to everyone, consider a regifting Secret Santa, where participants gift items they already own but are in good condition. This is both sustainable and economical.

The Secret Santa tradition encapsulates the spirit of the holidays—sharing, giving, and connecting. By focusing on thoughtfulness rather than monetary value, it reminds us that the real essence of gift-giving is in the gesture, not the price tag. Whether in tight financial times or just for the joy of simplicity, Secret

Santa is a cherished tradition that ensures everyone feels included and appreciated.

Teach Kids About Value: Lessons Beyond Materialism During the Holidays

The holiday season, with its shimmering lights, festive decorations, and allure of gift-giving, offers a unique opportunity to impart crucial life lessons to children. In an era where materialism often overshadows the true essence of celebrations, teaching children about the value of things beyond just their price tags can shape their perspectives and values for a lifetime.

Why Address Materialism with Kids?

1. **Long-term Perspective**: Children who understand the concept of value beyond just monetary terms grow up to be more financially responsible, empathetic, and less susceptible to peer pressure and consumerism.

2. **Gratitude and Contentment**: Recognizing the non-material blessings in life fosters a sense of gratitude and contentment, reducing the constant craving for 'more'.

3. **Deepened Relationships**: Children learn to value time, experiences, and memories shared with loved ones over material possessions, leading to deeper interpersonal connections.

Ways to Teach Children About Value During the Holidays:

1. **Share Stories**: Narrate tales from your childhood, when perhaps things were different, or share global stories that highlight different ways people celebrate. This broadens their worldview and helps them appreciate what they have.

2. **Gift-making**: Encourage children to make gifts rather than buy them. This could be crafts, handwritten letters, or baked goods. The effort and thought invested often make these gifts more special.

3. **Family Activities**: Prioritize family activities over shopping. Board games, baking sessions, movie nights, or just sharing stories can be both fun and bonding.

4. **Charitable Acts**: Engage in charitable activities as a family—whether it's donating toys, volunteering at a soup kitchen, or sponsoring a meal. It emphasizes the spirit of giving and compassion.

5. **Budgeting Exercise**: If they want something expensive, involve them in budgeting. Let them see how savings are done and the sacrifices that might be needed to afford certain items.

6. **Gift of Time**: Create homemade coupons offering your time—like a day out, a special storytelling session, or an evening of stargazing. This reinforces the idea that time spent together is invaluable.

7. **Focus on Traditions**: Uphold and explain family traditions, be it decorating the tree together, singing carols, or visiting a certain place every year. It helps children understand that consistency and memories are more important than the grandeur or cost of celebrations.

8. **Open Conversations**: Speak openly about financial realities without burdening them. This

can be a good introduction to understanding the value of money and the difference between wants and needs.

9. **Emphasize Non-Material Gifts**: Highlight the non-material gifts people offer—like support, kindness, love, and laughter. Discuss the joy derived from these intangible gifts.

10. **Experiences Over Things**: Instead of physical gifts, occasionally opt for experiences—like a visit to the zoo, a nature hike, or a day at the museum. Experiences often lead to lasting memories.

11. **Practice Gratitude**: Encourage children to list things they're grateful for. This simple act shifts focus from what they desire to what they already possess and cherish.

12. **Gift Wrapping Activity**: Use recycled materials or newspapers to wrap gifts. It not only teaches sustainability but also shows that it's the content and intent of the gift that matters, not the external appearance.

Incorporating lessons on value during the holidays lays the foundation for a balanced, grounded, and contented outlook towards life. By instilling these values early on, children are better equipped to navigate a world often dominated by materialistic pursuits, finding joy and satisfaction in the simpler, deeper facets of life.

Avoid High-Interest Debt: Navigating the Temptations of Holiday Spending

As the holiday season approaches, so does the enticing shimmer of storefronts, the appeal of online deals, and the emotional drive to ensure everyone on our gift list feels cherished. In such moments, credit cards can seem like a convenient answer, allowing us to stretch our purchasing power beyond our current means. However, the allure of easy credit can be deceptive, and without careful management, we may find ourselves sinking into the quagmire of high-interest debt.

Understanding the Pitfalls of High-Interest Debt:

1. **Compounding Interest**: The charm of credit cards often lies in the ability to make minimal payments. However, the remaining balance doesn't stay stagnant. Interest compounds, meaning you could end up paying interest on the interest.

2. **Long-term Financial Implications**: What starts as a seemingly manageable debt can balloon over time. The longer it takes to pay off, the more you end up paying in total.

3. **Credit Score Impact**: Maintaining a high balance or missing payments can negatively affect your credit score, making future financial endeavors, like getting a loan or a mortgage, more challenging and potentially more expensive.

Strategies to Minimize High-Interest Debt During the Holidays:

1. **Set a Clear Budget**: Before the holiday shopping season begins, establish a clear budget that you can comfortably afford without resorting to credit. Stick to this budget, resisting impulsive purchases.

2. **Cash Over Credit**: Use cash or a debit card for purchases. This ensures you're only spending money you actually have.

3. **Selective Credit Usage**: If you must use a credit card, do so judiciously. Consider using it for

larger, essential purchases, and avoid splurging on non-essentials.

4. **Understand Your Credit Card Terms**: Familiarize yourself with your card's interest rate, grace period, and any potential fees. Some cards might offer interest-free periods, which could be beneficial if you're confident in your ability to repay within that timeframe.

5. **Plan Repayments**: If you do end up using credit, have a concrete plan to pay off the balance as quickly as possible. Determine a set amount to pay each month that is above the minimum required payment.

6. **Avoid Store Credit Offers**: Retailers often entice shoppers with instant store credit offers that come with discounts. While tempting, these can carry high interest rates and hidden fees.

7. **Prioritize Payments**: If you have multiple debts, focus on paying off the highest interest ones first. This strategy reduces the total amount you'll end up paying in interest.

8. **Limit the Number of Cards**: The more credit cards you have, the harder it becomes to track and manage debt. Stick to one or two major credit cards and avoid opening new ones impulsively.

9. **Review Regularly**: Regularly review your credit card statements. This not only helps in tracking your spending but also in identifying any unauthorized transactions.

10. **Seek Counseling**: If you find yourself struggling with credit card debt, consider seeking financial counseling. Many non-profits offer services to help individuals navigate their financial challenges.

11. **Emergency Fund**: If possible, try to establish an emergency fund throughout the year. Even a small reserve can be immensely helpful during the holiday season, reducing your reliance on credit.

The essence of the holidays isn't found in extravagant gifts or opulent celebrations, but in the moments shared with loved ones, the memories created, and the warmth of togetherness. By navigating our finances mindfully, we can ensure that the post-holiday season is greeted with joy and contentment, rather than the dread of mounting bills.

Free Festivities: Embracing the Holiday Spirit on a Budget

The holiday season, with its warmth and cheer, beckons us to immerse in its festivities. Yet, despite the commercialized nature of modern celebrations, the true essence of the holidays isn't bound by price tags. Many communities, recognizing the importance of togetherness and shared joy, offer a plethora of free activities and events that capture the spirit of the season.

Benefits of Free Local Festivities:

1. **Cost-Effective Celebrations**: Obviously, free events save money, allowing you to enjoy the holidays without straining your budget.

2. **Community Bonding**: Attending local events fosters a sense of community, allowing neighbors to connect and share in the collective celebration.

3. **Authentic Experiences**: Local festivities often reflect the unique culture, traditions, and spirit

of a community, providing an authentic and meaningful experience.

4. **Reduced Stress**: Without the pressures of ticket bookings, reservations, or costs, you can spontaneously decide to participate in local events, making holiday planning more flexible and less stressful.

Examples of Free Festivities:

1. **Parades**: Many towns and cities host holiday parades, complete with marching bands, floats, and sometimes even a special appearance by Santa Claus himself.

2. **Light Displays**: Neighborhoods or local businesses often put up stunning light displays or decorations, turning a simple evening walk into a magical experience.

3. **Tree Lighting Ceremonies**: The annual lighting of the community Christmas tree can be a heartwarming event, often accompanied by music, caroling, and sometimes refreshments.

4. **Holiday Markets**: While shopping might cost money, simply wandering through festive holiday markets, soaking in the ambiance, and enjoying free samples or performances can be delightful.

5. **Caroling**: Join or listen to groups that go door-to-door singing classic holiday songs. Some communities even organize mass caroling events in parks or town squares.

6. **Church Events**: Many churches host nativity plays, choir performances, or candlelight services open to the entire community.

7. **Craft Workshops**: Some community centers or libraries might offer free holiday-themed craft workshops for kids and adults.

8. **Festive Storytelling**: Local libraries or bookstores occasionally host festive storytelling sessions for children, replete with holiday tales and legends.

9. **Ice Sculpture Displays**: In colder regions, it's not uncommon for artists to showcase intricate ice sculptures in public spaces.

10. **Window Shopping**: While it sounds mundane, the holiday-themed window displays of shops can be incredibly creative and a visual treat.

11. **Community Potlucks**: Some communities or neighborhoods organize potluck dinners, where the emphasis is on sharing and togetherness rather than extravagance.

12. **Outdoor Activities**: In snowy areas, simple pleasures like building snowmen, sledding, or engaging in snowball fights can be sources of free fun.

Making the Most of Free Festivities:

1. **Stay Informed**: Regularly check community bulletin boards, local newspapers, or community websites to stay updated on upcoming events.

2. **Participate Actively**: Don't just be a spectator. Engage in activities, volunteer, or even help organize events if you can.

3. **Invite Friends and Family**: Share the experience with loved ones. Inviting friends or family members can amplify the joy of attending free events.

4. **Dress Appropriately**: Ensure you're dressed comfortably for outdoor events, especially in colder regions. Layering up and wearing comfortable shoes can make the experience more enjoyable.

5. **Document the Experience**: Capture memories with photos or videos. Not only does this serve as a reminder of good times, but it can also be a great way to share the spirit with those who couldn't attend.

In essence, the holiday season is a time for reflection, joy, and connection. By seeking out and participating in free local festivities, we are reminded that the most memorable moments aren't necessarily the most expensive ones, but those that resonate with our hearts and foster a sense of community and shared happiness.

Shop Second Hand: The Art of Finding Treasures on a Budget

In the midst of a consumer-driven world where newness is often equated with value, there lies a world of untapped potential in second-hand marketplaces. Shopping second hand not only helps the wallet but also supports sustainable practices by reducing waste and giving items a second life. Especially during the holiday season, when budgets can be tight and the drive to find unique gifts is high, thrift stores and online marketplaces become invaluable resources.

Advantages of Second-Hand Shopping:

1. **Cost Savings**: One of the most evident advantages is the substantial savings. Items often sell for a fraction of their original price, allowing you to find quality products within a limited budget.

2. **Eco-friendly**: By buying second-hand, you reduce the demand for new products, which in

turn decreases the environmental impacts of manufacturing and transportation.

3. **Unique Finds**: Thrift stores and second-hand markets are treasure troves of unique items, vintage pieces, and one-of-a-kind finds that can make for memorable gifts.

4. **Higher Quality**: Often, for the same price as a new but lower-quality item, you can find a high-quality, gently used item that has withstood the test of time.

5. **Supporting Local**: Buying from local thrift shops or sellers can support your local community, especially if the thrift shop is linked to charitable organizations.

Tips for Successful Second-Hand Shopping:

1. **Know What You're Looking For**: Have an idea or a list of items you're seeking. This will help you stay focused and reduce impulse purchases.

2. **Inspect Items Thoroughly**: Check for damages, stains, or signs of excessive wear. Remember that some issues, like missing buttons, can be

easily fixed, while others might be deal-breakers.

3. **Be Patient**: Second-hand shopping is like a treasure hunt; it requires patience. Visit multiple stores or check online platforms regularly for new listings.

4. **Research Online Marketplaces**: Websites like eBay, Poshmark, and Facebook Marketplace can be gold mines for second-hand goods. Make sure to read item descriptions carefully and check seller ratings.

5. **Haggle Politely**: In some second-hand settings, especially at garage sales or certain online marketplaces, it's acceptable to negotiate prices. Do so respectfully.

6. **Understand Return Policies**: Some thrift stores have strict no-return policies, while online platforms might offer buyer protection. Always inquire beforehand.

7. **Sanitize and Clean**: Once you've bought an item, ensure you clean or sanitize it

appropriately, whether it's washing clothes or wiping down hard goods.

8. **Stay Safe Online**: If purchasing from online marketplaces where you meet the seller in person, choose public meeting places and let someone know where you're going.

9. **Gift Presentation**: Just because an item is second-hand doesn't mean it can't be presented beautifully. Use creative wrapping or packaging to make your gift feel special.

10. **Stay Open-minded**: Sometimes, you'll come across items you hadn't considered but are perfect for someone on your list. Being flexible and open to possibilities can yield unexpected rewards.

Shopping second hand, when approached with enthusiasm and an open mind, can transform the holiday gift-giving experience. Not only does it offer an opportunity to find exceptional items at affordable prices, but it also promotes sustainable consumer behavior. When gifting a second-hand item, you're not just offering a tangible object but also a story, a piece of history, and a testament to the idea that value isn't just about brand-new price tags.

Embrace Minimalism: Finding Depth in Simplicity This Holiday Season

The holiday season, often characterized by opulence and excess, can sometimes overshadow the genuine sentiments of love, togetherness, and gratitude. Minimalism, as a philosophy and lifestyle, urges us to pare down to the essentials, to seek quality over quantity, and to find joy in simplicity. By embracing minimalism during the holidays, we allow ourselves to focus on what truly matters, creating a celebration that's both meaningful and sustainable.

Benefits of a Minimalist Holiday:

1. **Reduced Stress**: Simplifying your holidays can significantly reduce the pressure of shopping, decorating, and planning elaborate events, giving you more time to relax and enjoy the season.

2. **Financial Savings**: Cutting back on extravagant purchases means fewer financial strains,

allowing you to start the new year without the burden of holiday debt.

3. **Deeper Connections**: With fewer distractions, you can devote more time and attention to loved ones, nurturing relationships and creating lasting memories.

4. **Environmental Impact**: A minimalist approach often results in less waste from packaging, decorations, and unused items, promoting a greener holiday season.

5. **Greater Appreciation**: By focusing on fewer but more meaningful gifts and activities, you cultivate a deeper appreciation for what you have and receive.

Steps to Cultivate a Minimalist Holiday:

1. **Reflect on Traditions**: Ask yourself which holiday traditions genuinely resonate with you and your family. It might be time to let go of certain practices that no longer serve a purpose or to introduce new, simpler ones.

2. **Limit Gifts**: Consider the "Four Gift Rule" for each person: something they want, something they need, something to wear, and something to read. This approach can simplify shopping and ensure that each gift is thoughtful.

3. **Simplify Decor**: Instead of decking every corner of your home, choose a few key areas to decorate. Often, a few well-placed items can evoke the holiday spirit just as effectively as an all-out display.

4. **Quality Over Quantity**: Whether it's gifts, food, or activities, focus on quality. A few well-chosen events or gifts can be more memorable than a packed schedule or a mountain of presents.

5. **Digital Detox**: Allocate certain times during the holidays to unplug. Use this time to engage in face-to-face conversations, read a book, or simply enjoy the peace.

6. **Experience Over Things**: Gift experiences like a day out, a class, or a workshop. These often leave more lasting memories than physical objects.

7. **Handmade and Heartfelt**: Handwritten letters, homemade crafts, or baked goods often have a personal touch that store-bought items can't replicate.

8. **Mindful Consumption**: Be conscious of where and how you shop. Support local artisans or buy sustainable products, reflecting a commitment to mindful consumption.

9. **Declutter Before the Holidays**: Make it a tradition to declutter before the festive season. Donate items you no longer need. This creates space, both physically and mentally, for the holidays.

10. **Set Boundaries**: It's okay to say no. Whether it's turning down an invitation or opting out of a gift exchange, prioritize your well-being and peace of mind.

Conclusion: Embracing minimalism during the holidays isn't about forgoing joy or celebration. Instead, it's a conscious choice to strip away the unnecessary, redirecting focus towards the core values of the season. By simplifying our approach, we often find that the essence of the holidays—love, gratitude, and connection—shines brighter than ever.

Seek Assistance: Leaning on Community During the Holiday Season

The holiday season, for all its glitter and joy, can sometimes amplify feelings of loneliness, stress, and financial strain. It's important to recognize that everyone, at some point in their lives, might need a helping hand. Whether you're facing financial challenges, seeking emotional support, or just need a sense of belonging, community organizations and religious groups often rally to provide assistance during this time. Embracing this support is not a sign of weakness but of strength in recognizing when help is needed.

Benefits of Seeking Assistance:

1. **Alleviating Financial Strain**: Many organizations offer food baskets, toys for children, and even assistance with utility bills during the colder months. This can significantly ease the financial burden of the holidays.

2. **Emotional Support**: Beyond tangible aid, being part of a community event or gathering can provide emotional and psychological support, reducing feelings of isolation.

3. **Building Community Ties**: Participating in community events, even as a recipient of assistance, can help strengthen connections within your local community, fostering a sense of belonging.

4. **Resource Sharing**: Community centers often have information on various resources available, from job boards to free educational workshops, counseling services, and more.

Steps to Access Community Support:

1. **Research Local Organizations**: Start by looking up local charities, nonprofits, or religious groups. They often have specific holiday programs designed to assist those in need.

2. **Visit Community Centers**: These hubs often have bulletin boards or staff who are informed about upcoming events, drives, and assistance programs.

3. **Reach Out Early**: Many assistance programs have registration deadlines. It's advisable to reach out well in advance to ensure you don't miss out.

4. **Be Honest About Your Needs**: When seeking assistance, be clear about what you need. Whether it's food, gifts for your children, or utility assistance, transparency helps organizations provide the best support.

5. **Volunteer**: If you're able, consider giving back by volunteering. This not only provides a sense of purpose but can also connect you with resources and like-minded individuals.

6. **Connect with Religious Institutions**: Churches, mosques, temples, and other religious institutions often have outreach programs during the holidays, providing everything from meals to counseling.

7. **Look for Local Online Groups**: Platforms like Facebook or Nextdoor often have community groups where members share resources,

events, and sometimes even organize assistance for fellow members.

8. **Attend Workshops or Classes**: Some community organizations offer free workshops on budgeting, job searching, or other skills that can be invaluable during challenging times.

9. **Seek Counseling**: The holidays can be emotionally challenging. Some community groups offer free or sliding-scale counseling services.

10. **Remember Confidentiality**: Many organizations understand the importance of privacy. If you're hesitant to seek assistance due to concerns about confidentiality, know that many groups prioritize discretion.

Conclusion: Seeking assistance during the holidays, or at any time, is a testament to human resilience and the understanding that everyone needs support at times. The community spirit, especially during the festive season, underscores the importance of togetherness, understanding, and compassion. Remember, the act of reaching out not only benefits you but also strengthens the fabric of the community as a whole, reinforcing the idea that we are better together.

Communicate: Honesty as the Cornerstone of Fulfilling Holidays

Open communication, especially during financially challenging times, is paramount. The holidays, rife with expectations and sometimes pressures, can compound these challenges. Being transparent about your financial situation with loved ones can lead to mutual understanding, innovative solutions, and, more importantly, deepen the emotional bonds by showcasing vulnerability and trust.

Benefits of Open Communication:

1. **Shared Understanding**: By being honest about your financial situation, you allow family and friends to empathize and adjust expectations accordingly.

2. **Reduced Stress**: Discussing budget constraints can help alleviate the internal stress of meeting perceived expectations and prevent overspending.

3. **Collective Creativity**: When the whole group is aware of budget limitations, it often leads to

more creative and collaborative solutions for holiday celebrations.

4. **Strengthened Bonds**: Genuine conversations about challenges can foster deeper connections and mutual support among loved ones.

5. **Shared Burden**: You might discover that others are in a similar boat. Knowing you're not alone can provide emotional relief and pave the way for collective problem-solving.

Steps to Effective Communication:

1. **Choose the Right Time**: Initiate the conversation when everyone is relaxed and free from distractions. It might be during a casual family dinner or a weekend afternoon.

2. **Be Honest but Positive**: Approach the topic with honesty but also emphasize the positives, like the desire to have a meaningful holiday celebration regardless of financial constraints.

3. **Use "I" Statements**: Frame your feelings in personal terms to prevent others from becoming defensive. For example, "I feel

stressed about the upcoming expenses" instead of "You always expect expensive gifts."

4. **Suggest Alternatives**: When discussing limitations, also offer potential solutions like handmade gifts, potluck dinners, or other budget-friendly holiday ideas.

5. **Listen Actively**: Give others a chance to share their feelings and ideas. Active listening involves being present, avoiding interruptions, and acknowledging the other person's point of view.

6. **Avoid Blame**: The aim is to find solutions and garner support, not assign blame. Avoid statements that might make others feel guilty or responsible.

7. **Establish New Traditions**: Use the opportunity to introduce new holiday traditions that are less about spending and more about spending time together.

8. **Set Clear Expectations**: If there's a gift exchange, set a clear budget. If you're hosting, let guests know if it's a potluck. Clarity can prevent misunderstandings.

9. **Encourage Feedback**: Ask for input from family and friends on how to make the holidays special within a budget. Collective brainstorming can yield wonderful results.

10.   **Reiterate Love and Appreciation**: Remind your loved ones that the essence of the season is about love, gratitude, and togetherness. Material aspects, though enjoyable, are secondary.

Conclusion: The holiday season, at its core, is about unity, love, and the joy of togetherness. By communicating openly with loved ones about financial constraints, you pave the way for more genuine, heartfelt celebrations. In doing so, you might find that the most memorable aspects of the holidays aren't the expensive gifts or lavish feasts, but the laughter, stories, and shared moments that cost nothing but are truly priceless.

Stay Positive: Cherishing the True Essence of the Holidays

The holiday season, with its twinkling lights and merry carols, holds a magic that goes beyond material possessions. While it's easy to get lost in the commercialism, staying grounded in the true essence of the holidays—love, gratitude, and togetherness—can bring more fulfillment than any store-bought gift. Adopting a positive outlook and centering yourself in these core values is a vital way to keep the season joyful, even amidst financial strains or other challenges.

Benefits of Staying Positive:

1. **Enhanced Well-being**: A positive mindset has been linked to improved mental and emotional well-being. Emphasizing love and gratitude can elevate mood and reduce stress.

2. **Strengthened Relationships**: By focusing on togetherness rather than materialism, you can deepen bonds with loved ones, creating memories that last a lifetime.

3. **Shifted Perspective**: A positive outlook can help you see the silver linings, allowing you to appreciate the small joys and blessings in your life.

4. **Increased Resilience**: When you center on gratitude and love, you're better equipped to handle challenges and setbacks, using them as opportunities for growth.

5. **Promotion of Generosity**: Embracing a positive, grateful mindset often leads to acts of kindness, fostering a sense of community and interconnectedness.

Ways to Maintain Positivity:

1. **Daily Gratitude Journal**: Set aside a few minutes each day to jot down things you're thankful for. Over time, this practice can shift your focus from what you lack to what you have.

2. **Mindfulness and Meditation**: Engage in mindfulness practices or meditation to stay present and savor the joyous moments.

3. **Limit Exposure to Consumerism**: Reduce the time spent on activities that push commercialism, such as excessive shopping or watching holiday sales ads.

4. **Engage in Acts of Kindness**: Acts, big or small, can generate a sense of happiness and fulfillment. Consider volunteering or even just performing small acts of kindness for neighbors, friends, or strangers.

5. **Reconnect with Nature**: Take walks or spend time outside. Nature has a grounding effect, helping you disconnect from materialism and reconnect with the world's natural beauty.

6. **Create DIY Decorations**: Engage in crafting or making decorations. The act of creating can be therapeutic and serves as a reminder that joy can come from simple, handmade things.

7. **Engage in Positive Affirmations**: Start your day with positive affirmations or quotes that resonate with the holiday spirit and your values.

8. **Limit Comparisons**: Remember that everyone's journey is different. Avoid comparing your

celebrations or gifts to others, especially in the age of social media.

9. **Celebrate Small Wins**: Find joy in the small moments and achievements, be it baking a perfect holiday treat or having a heartwarming conversation with a loved one.

10.   **Seek Support**: If you find it challenging to stay positive, reach out. This could be friends, family, or professionals who can provide perspective and support.

Conclusion: The holidays, in their truest form, are a celebration of love, unity, and gratitude. While gifts, decorations, and feasts add to the festivity, they are but accessories to the core spirit of the season. By focusing on intangible gifts—warm embraces, shared laughter, stories recounted by the fireplace, and the joy of simply being with loved ones—you can ensure that your holiday experience is rich, meaningful, and deeply fulfilling. Remember, it's not about what's under the tree but who's around it.